Pricked Pinkies

Readers' Theater
How to Put on a Production

A Readers' Theater
Script and Guide

By Nancy K. Wallace • Illustrated by Nina Mata

magic
wagon

visit us at www.abdopublishing.com

To my daughters, Mollie and Elizabeth, who have spent endless hours helping with library plays! —NKW

Printed in the United States of America, North Mankato, Minnesota.
042013
092013
♻ This book contains at least 10% recycled materials.

Written by Nancy K. Wallace
Illustrations by Nina Mata
Edited by Stephanie Hedlund and Rochelle Baltzer
Cover and interior design by Renée LaViolette

Library of Congress Cataloging-in-Publication Data

Wallace, Nancy K.
  Pricked pinkies : a readers' theater script and guide / by Nancy K. Wallace ; illustrated by Nina Mata.
    pages cm. -- (Readers' theater: how to put on a production)
  ISBN 978-1-61641-987-5
1. Fairy tales--Adaptations--Juvenile drama. 2. Theater--Production and direction--Juvenile literature.
3. Readers' theater--Juvenile literature. I. Mata, Nina, 1981- illustrator. II. Title.
  PS3623.A4436P85 2013
  812'.6--dc23
                        2013006051

Table of Contents

School Plays

Do you like to act, make props, create weird sound effects, or paint scenery? You should put on a production. Plays are lots of fun! And a play is a great way for kids to work together as a team.

A readers' theater production can be done very simply. You just read your lines. You don't have to memorize them! An adapted readers' theater production looks more like a regular play. The performers wear makeup and costumes. The stage has scenery and props. The cast moves around to show the action. But, performers can still read their scripts.

To hold a production, you will need a large space. An auditorium with a stage is ideal. A classroom will work, too. Now, choose a date and get permission to use the space.

Finally, make flyers or posters to advertise your play. Place them around your school and community. Tell your friends and family. Everyone enjoys watching kids perform!

Cast & Crew

There are many people needed to put on a production. First, decide who will play each part. Each person in the cast will need a script. All the performers should practice their lines.

Pricked Pinkies has a lot of speaking parts.

Narrator - The storyteller

Mouse - Sits beside the narrator

King - Princess Elizabeth's father

Queen - Princess Elizabeth's mother

Esmeralda - The bad fairy

Lily - The good fairy

Princess Elizabeth - The king and queen's daughter

Prince Charming - Princess Elizabeth's boyfriend

Party Guests - Choose at least four guests but you can include as many as you like

Next, a crew is needed. The show can't go on without these important people! Some jobs can be combined. Every show needs a director. This person organizes everything and everyone in the show.

The director works with the production crew. This includes the costume designers, who borrow or make all the costumes. Stage managers make sure things run smoothly.

Your production can also have a stage crew. This includes lighting designers to run spotlights and other lighting. Set designers plan and make scenery. The special effects crew takes care of sound and other unusual effects.

Sets & Props

At a readers' theater production, the performers sit on stools at the front of the room. But, an adapted readers' theater production or full play requires some sets and props.

Sets include a background for each scene of the play. Props are things you'll need during the play. *Pricked Pinkies* could have the following set and props:

Scene Set - All of the scenes take place in the castle. You can paint sheets of cardboard to look like stone walls. Change the props for each scene to make the walls look like they are in different rooms.

Props - The party scene will need a table with dishes. The attic scenes will need a spinning wheel and an armchair. You can make magic wands from decorated pencils or wooden dowels. A cradle and doll are needed. The party can have glasses filled with colored water or real punch and other food.

One of the main props is the spinning wheel. Borrow a spinning wheel, if possible. It will make your set look great! If you can't borrow one, paint a spinning wheel on cardboard.

You'll also need tickets that list important information. Be sure to include the title of the play and where it will take place. List the date and time of your performance.

Your production can also have a playbill. It is a printed program. The front of a playbill has the title, date, and time of the play. Playbills list all of the cast and production team inside.

Makeup & Costumes

The stage and props aren't the only things people will be looking at in your play. The makeup artist has a big job. Stage makeup needs to be brighter than regular makeup. Even boys wear stage makeup!

Costume designers set the scene just as much as set designers. They borrow costumes or adapt old clothing for each character. For example, make a cloak out of a length of fabric gathered at the neck. Ask adults if you need help finding or sewing costumes.

Pricked Pinkies performers will need these costumes:

Narrator - A shirt and pants with a cloak

Mouse - A gray or brown sweat suit, a headband with ears, and face paint for whiskers and a nose

King - A crown, a fancy shirt, and black pants

Queen - A crown and a fancy dress

Esmeralda - A black dress and fairy wings

Lily - A pink or purple dress and fairy wings

Princess Elizabeth - A small crown and a fancy dress

Prince Charming - A small crown, a fancy shirt, and black pants
Party Guests - Girls should wear fancy dresses and boys should
wear fancy shirts and plain pants

Stage Directions

When your sets, props, and costumes are ready, it is important to rehearse. Choose a time that everyone can attend. Try to have at least five or six rehearsals before your show.

You should practice together as a team even if you will be reading your scripts for readers' theater. A play should sound like a conversation. Try to avoid pauses when no one is speaking. You can do this by adding sound effects.

Some theater terms may seem strange. The *wings* are the sides of the stage that the audience can't see. The *house* is where the audience sits. The *curtains* refers to the main curtain at the front of the stage.

When reading your script, the stage directions are in parentheses. They are given from the performer's point of view. You will be facing the audience when you are performing. Left will be on your left and right will be on your right. When rehearsing, perform the stage directions and the lines to get used to moving around the stage.

Script: *Pricked Pinkies*

(Opening curtain: The narrator sits stage right on a stool with the mouse close by. The king and the queen are bending over the cradle at center stage.)

Narrator: *(Clears his throat before speaking)* **Scene 1 — The Castle.** Once upon a time, there was a beautiful princess . . .

Mouse: *(Taps his foot and sighs)* Why do fairy tales always start that way? I understand the "once upon a time" part. But why are fairy tales always about princesses?

Narrator: Because people like stories about princesses. Some of the best stories I've ever heard were about princesses!

Mouse: *(Taps his foot and looks angry)* I think there should be more stories about mice! Is there a mouse in this story?

Narrator: Would you like me to put a mouse in the story?

Mouse: *(Jumping up and down)* Oh yes, please!

Narrator: Okay, I will. But you'll have to be quiet and listen.

Mouse: I will be as quiet as a mouse.

Narrator: That's not saying much. Some mice are not quiet at all! *(He clears his throat loudly.)* Let me begin again. Once upon a time, there was a princess and a mouse.

Mouse: *(Jumping up and down again)* Oh, the mouse is at the very beginning! I love this story!

Narrator: Now, the princess's name was Elizabeth. She was very beautiful. On the day she was born, her parents decided to have a party in her honor.

King: I am so happy that we have a little daughter! Let's have a party!

Queen: That sounds like an excellent idea, my dear. I'll have Cook look up her finest recipes!

King: And ask her to make a huge cake!

Mouse: They should make a cake shaped like a mouse! That's a really good idea!

Narrator: *(Putting his finger to his lips)* Shhh, don't interrupt!

King: We'll invite all the important people in the kingdom!

Queen: I'll have the jester send out the invitations tomorrow.

Mouse: Wait a minute! Aren't jesters supposed to make jokes? Why would the queen give an important job like sending invitations to a jester?

Narrator: Maybe everyone else was busy. Anyway, that's how the story is told. You are right, it wasn't a good idea. The jester forgot to send an invitation to Fairy Esmeralda. She was *very* angry.

Mouse: *(Nodding)* I knew it!

(The king and queen exit stage right. The party guests enter. One moves the cradle to the center stage. Some people bend over to admire the baby. Others talk in small groups. Music plays in the background.)

Narrator: **Scene 2 — The Castle.** On the day of the party, everyone gathered at the castle. There was lots of food and everyone brought presents to the baby princess.

Mouse: Where was the mouse?

Narrator: I'm getting to that part. He was hiding in the princess's cradle so he could protect her. Now, let me get back to the story.

Mouse: Don't let me stop you!

Narrator: Just when everyone was having a very good time, Fairy Esmeralda flew into the room.

(Esmeralda enters from stage right. The guests move away from her.)

Mouse: Oh, man! I'll bet she wasn't in a good mood. It stinks when you are the only one who isn't invited to a party!

Narrator: You're right. She was very angry! Instead of bringing a present, she brought a terrible curse to put on the little baby.

Mouse: You're kidding! How rude!

Esmeralda: *(Waves her magic wand and looks at the king and queen. She begins to laugh.)* Today, you laugh. Tomorrow, you'll cry! At sweet sixteen, your daughter will die!

King: How dare you! Guards, seize that woman!

Esmeralda: *(Laughs again)* The spell is cast! On your daughter's sixteenth birthday, she will prick her finger on a spindle and fall down dead!

Mouse: Hold it! I don't understand. What's a spindle?

Narrator: It's part of a spinning wheel. Now, listen!

King: *(Pointing at Esmeralda)* Take that woman to the dungeon!

Queen: *(Picks up the baby doll and holds her)* Oh, my beautiful daughter! What shall we do?

Narrator: But just then the mouse jumped up.

Mouse: *(Jumping up and spreading his arms)* Ta-da! *(Then, he hesitates)* Wait a minute, what did he do?

Narrator: He vowed to protect the princess!

Mouse: Oh! *(Stands up and throws out his arms)* I vow to protect the princess! I'll chew off the end of every spindle in the castle!

Narrator: Hey, that's actually not a bad idea!

Mouse: Thank you! What happened then?

Narrator: Well, the king tried to have Esmeralda thrown into the dungeon, but she flew away. *(Esmeralda flaps her arms and flies off stage.)* No one could catch her.

Mouse: Weren't there any good fairies at the party?

Narrator: There was one. Her name was Lily.

Lily: *(Stepping close to the queen and the baby)* No one can break a curse once it is cast. But I *can* change it. *(She waves her wand.)* Should the spindle harm her finger, only sleep, not death, will linger. None can spoil her birthday's bliss. She will wake to true love's kiss!

(All the party guests leave the stage. Just the mouse and narrator remain.)

Mouse: *(Clasps hands in front of chest)* Everything will be okay, right?

Narrator: Well, the king and queen tried very hard to make everything okay. For fifteen years, they banished every spinning wheel in the castle.

Mouse: I thought the mouse was going to chew all the tops off.

Narrator: He did. But sadly, he got a splinter in his throat and . . .

Mouse: (*Gasping and putting his hands to his throat*) Oh, my gosh! Choking! Choking!

Narrator: Knock it off! Do you want to hear this story or not? Be quiet or I'll write you out of the story!

Mouse: (*Sits very still and puts hands over mouth*) My lips are sealed.

Narrator: They better be or you are out of here! Now listen, we're coming to the exciting part.

(*The king is pacing back and forth across the stage. The queen is standing to one side with Princess Elizabeth.*)

Narrator: **Scene 3 — The Castle.** Now on Princess Elizabeth's sixteenth birthday, the king was very worried. He was afraid that Fairy Esmeralda's curse would come true! He barred the doors and windows of the castle. No one but his most trusted household staff was allowed inside.

Princess: Papa, I don't understand. Why can't I have a birthday party? Turning sixteen is important! I want to see my friends!

Queen: We'll have a party next year, dear.

Princess: Couldn't I just invite Prince Charming to dinner? He won't be any trouble at all.

King: No, my dear. Now run along and amuse yourself until dinner. Cook is baking a delicious cake for you.

Princess: *(Sadly)* Oh, all right.

(King, queen, and Princess Elizabeth exit. Esmeralda enters the stage with a spinning wheel. There is an old armchair in the corner.)

Narrator: **Scene 4 — The Attic.** And so the princess wandered through the deserted halls of the castle feeling very sad. *(Princess enters stage left)* Finally, she came to a room in the attic that she had never been in before. In the room, there was an old woman spinning yarn.

Mouse: Oh, Princess Elizabeth! Stop! Stay away from her! She's that old hag who cursed you!

Princess: Who are you?

Esmeralda: *(In a kind voice)* Just an old woman, my dear. My name isn't important. Why do you look so sad on such a beautiful day?

Princess: Today is my birthday and my father won't let me have a party.

Esmeralda: Well, that's not very nice of him. I'll bet that you are sixteen

years old, too! Sweet sixteen is a very special birthday!

Princess: Yes, I am sixteen! How did you know that?

Esmeralda: Oh, I just have a feeling about such things. Why don't you come and help me spin? It will pass the time.

Princess: I don't know anything about spinning.

Esmeralda: I'll be happy to teach you, dear. Just come a little closer!

Mouse: Princess Elizabeth, stay away from her! She is one *bad* fairy!

Narrator: The mouse did try to stop her. But Princess Elizabeth touched the spindle.

Princess: *(The princess reaches out toward the spinning wheel)* Ouch! *(Puts her hand to her head)* Oh my, I feel so strange.

Esmeralda: *(Pats the chair beside her)* Just sit down here, my dear.

Princess: Thank you. Maybe I'll just close my eyes for a minute.

Narrator: The princess fell into a deep sleep.

Esmeralda: Oh, I am bad and I am rotten! My name will never be forgotten! *(Esmeralda flaps her arms and runs out of the room.)*

Narrator: *(Looking at the mouse)* Well, you weren't much help! You vowed to protect the princess!

Mouse: So, what should I do now?

Narrator: Do you remember the spell that Fairy Lily cast? You must find the princess's true love.

Mouse: *(Looking puzzled)* Who is her true love?

Narrator: Prince Charming, of course!

Mouse: But the castle doors and windows are barred! How am I supposed to find him?

Narrator: I thought mice could slip through very tiny spaces. Now is your chance to save the day!

Mouse: You're right! I vowed to protect the princess! I will find Prince Charming and bring him back.

Narrator: And so the mouse ran down 17 staircases . . .

Mouse: *(Turns and looks at the narrator)* Seventeen! Geez! I could die of cardiac arrest! Who'll save the princess then?

(Mouse should mimic running downstairs but stay next to the narrator.)

Narrator: And then the mouse ran 15 miles and finally found Prince Charming . . .

Narrator: **Scene 5 — The Attic.** It wasn't until the gray light of morning that hoofbeats were heard on the road below the castle. Prince Charming had arrived at last!

(The king and queen are kneeling beside the princess. Mouse enters with Prince Charming.)

Mouse: *(Sounds disgusted)* With the poor, exhausted mouse in his pocket. Move over, Your Majesties! Help is on the way! All you have to do to break Esmeralda's curse is kiss her, Prince Charming!

Prince Charming: I would love to do that! *(Prince bends over the princess and pretends to kiss her.)*

Narrator: As soon as the prince kissed the princess, she woke up!

(Princess sits up and smiles at Prince Charming.)

Narrator: And they all lived happily . . .

Mouse: Wait! Wait! Wait! Tell the princess the part about how a tiny mouse ran 15 miles to save her life!

Princess: Did you really run all that way, just to save me? *(Mouse nods.)* You are a hero! I will ask my father to make you a knight.

Mouse: *(Acting embarrassed)* Really? I'm a hero? I mean—thanks! Oh my gosh, I'm going to be a real knight!

Narrator: And I thought you were hard to live with before!

King: I will make you Sir Mouse, the Brave. And I will give you enough cheese for you and your family for all the years of your life!

Mouse: Now that's a *good* story!

The End

Adapting Readers' Theater Scripts

Readers' theater can be done very simply. You just read your lines. You don't have to memorize them! Performers sit on chairs or stools. They read their parts without moving around.

Adapted Readers' Theater

This looks more like a regular play. The performers wear makeup and costumes. The stage has scenery and props. The cast moves around to show the action. Performers can still read their scripts.

Hold a Puppet Show

Some schools and libraries have puppet collections. Students make the puppets be the actors. They read their scripts.

Teacher's Guides

Readers' Theater Teacher's Guides are available online. Each guide includes reading levels for each character and additional production tips for each play. Visit Teacher's Guides at **www.abdopublishing.com** to get yours today!